St Hilda's Abbey

The tall headland at Whitby is an ancient holy place, among the most venerable in the kingdom. Even today, Whitby's parish church continues the tradition. It is a charming building of mixed date and unusual furnishings, well worth a visit in its own right. But it turns its back on the town of Whitby, to confront the stark skeleton of an abbey. Here on Whitby's headland was a burial-place of kings, repository of relics and training-ground of a galaxy of saints.

Whitby's cliffs have been sacred since 657, when Hilda, 'a most devoted servant of Christ', brought a community to re-settle the site of what may have been, in the twilight empire, a Roman coastal fort or signal station. We know a good deal about Hilda from the writings of Bede, the eighth-century Northumbrian ecclesiastical historian who provides a very full account of the saint's pious life and good works. Hilda was a pioneer of the Anglo-Saxon conversion to Christianity.

She had been ta[...] [...]ary to the North. Be[...] [...]s of Hartlepool, whe[...] [...] the monastic life[...] industry' to the double community of monks and nuns at Whitby, down the coast to the south. As Bede tells us:

> **S**he established the same **R**ule of life as in the other monastery [Hartlepool], teaching them to observe strictly the virtues of justice, devotion and chastity and other virtues too, but above all things to continue in peace and charity. **A**fter the example of the primitive church, no one was rich, no one was in need, for they had all things in common and none had any private property.
>
> (Bede, *Ecclesiastical History*)

These early standards were important, and they will be worth recalling in the context of Whitby's later development, far removed from the ideals of its foundress. In Abbess Hilda's own day, the outstanding reputation of her new community at Whitby brought the rival parties in the Northumbrian Church to the abbey in 664 for the Synod (Council) of Whitby. This famous meeting had been called to decide whether to adopt the Roman or the Celtic method of dating Easter and other matters in dispute between the two branches of Christianity in the country, which was threatening to split the English Church. King Oswy of Northumbria, patron of Hilda's abbey, had summoned the Synod, and it was left to him to resolve - with a smile, we are told - that the Roman tradition should triumph. His was a political decision in essence, but Oswy made a joke of it, pretending to fear Rome's patron, St Peter, as appointed key-holder of Heaven. 'I tell you', said Oswy, 'since he is the doorkeeper I will not contradict him . . . o t h e r w i s e when I come to the gates of the kingdom of heaven, there may be no one to open them because the one who on your showing holds the keys has turned his back on me.'

Late medieval stained-glass window showing St Hilda (Christ Church Cathedral, Oxford)

With this, the Celtic practices introduced into Northumbria by monks from the Scottish monastery of Iona retreated into the North, abandoning the field to the Roman Church of St Augustine's original mission (597-604) to Canterbury.

Whitby Abbey, until its destruction by the Danes, retained much of its original importance. After St Hilda, the next abbesses of Whitby were Enfleda, Oswy's widowed queen, and Elfleda, his daughter, both to become saints in their turn. Elfleda's grandfather Edwin, her father Oswy and mother Enfleda, were all to be buried at the family monastery at Whitby, the abbey becoming the principal mausoleum of the Northumbrian royal line and its adherents.

There was nothing unusual, in the English Church, in the double monastery (catering for both sexes) of St Hilda's foundation. There were established precedents for such houses on the Continent, and indeed the scholarship and piety of the English double monasteries, each ruled by an abbess, came to be widely renowned. Whitby's early years, under such leadership, were of singular distinction. Hilda had emphasised the value of learning, and her abbey became the school of bishops - Oftfor at Worcester, Bosa and Wilfrid at York, Aetla at Dorchester, and John at Hexham - 'all of them men of singular merit and holiness'. It was at Whitby too, on Hilda's personal initiative, that the poet Caedmon sheltered, 'who was specially marked out by the Grace of God, so that he used to compose godly and religious songs . . . in English, which was his own tongue'.

Hilda, Enfleda and Elfleda were not alone among Anglo-Saxon royal women in taking a leading role in contemporary monasticism. This panel painting of c.1400 shows a scene from the life of St Etheldreda, daughter of one king and wife of another, who founded a double monastery at Ely in 673

However, Bede tells the story also of the double house at Coldingham where things had not gone nearly as well. At his prayers one day, a monk at Coldingham, Adamnan, had been 'greatly startled' to find himself in the presence of a stranger who congratulated him warmly on a zeal plainly lacking elsewhere in the same community.

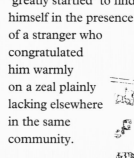

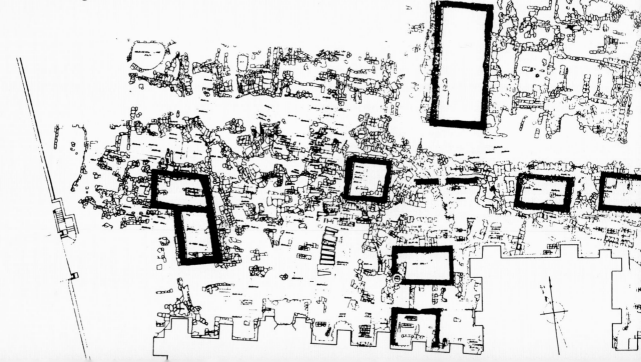

Coldingham was, in fact, to burn down not very much later.

The double community at Whitby came to a sudden end itself in 867, when the Danes invaded Northumbria. They 'spread themselves over the whole country and filled all with blood and grief; they destroyed the churches and monasteries far and wide with fire and sword, leaving nothing remaining save the bare unroofed walls'. Whitby went down with the rest, so that by the time of its resurrection in the post-Conquest period, there was nothing the Normans could employ from Hilda's buildings, even had it suited them to do so.

What we know of these early structures is limited. Bede, in his Coldingham narrative, talks of that monastery's 'lofty buildings'. But it is of the 'cells that were built for praying and for reading' that the Whitby evidence tells us more. Archaeological excavations at Whitby in the 1920s uncovered a group of such cells, north of the Norman church, laid out along paths in an orderly manner but none of them individually of great size. The many loomweights found in the area, not present at male monastic sites of comparable date more recently excavated at Monkwearmouth and Jarrow, suggest that these were the quarters of Whitby nuns, where they would have been engaged in spinning and weaving. From the same context, numerous objects of personal adornment imply a life-style, at least in the community's latter days, far removed from the prescriptions of St Hilda.

Coins in great numbers were recovered at Whitby. There were decorative objects of glass, bone and jet, with much ornamental metalwork (mainly of bronze but of silver also), including hanging bowls and cooking pans, writing tools and book mounts, discs, strap-ends, rings, brooches and buckles, pendants, pins, tweezers and hooks, with a small collection of keys. In Abbess Hilda's day, there had been no private property at Whitby. '*Let no one,*' St Benedict had ruled, '*have anything of his own, anything whatever, whether book or tablets or pen or whatever it may be; for monks should not have even their bodies and wills at their own disposal.*' Yet '*this most wicked vice,*' which '*especially ought to be utterly rooted out of the monastery,*' had infested Whitby by the ninth century, if not before, just as it had poisoned the community at Coldingham.

SCALE 24 FEET TO 1 INCH

Left: *Excavated remains of St Hilda's Abbey. Identifiable buildings are distinguished in darker tone, with the outline of the later church shown below.* Inset: *Some of the objects recovered in the excavations*

Whitby's Saints

Edwin *(d 633)*: King of Northumbria and husband of Ethelburga, the Kentish princess, who brought the missionary, Paulinus, to the North. Edwin's head, preserved at York, became the focus of a cult. But his body, 'revealed' to the monks of Whitby, was given a shrine at the abbey where it rested among the royal ladies of his line.

Hilda *(d 680)*: related to the royal lines of both Northumbria and East Anglia, and foundress of the double monastery at Whitby. Hilda's cult was strong in the North, but her bones had been removed to Glastonbury in the second quarter of the tenth century, and were accordingly not accessible to Whitby's monks, even after the post-Conquest re-foundation.

Caedmon *(d 680)*: A monk of Whitby, originally a herdsman, whose poetic gifts were recognised by Abbess Hilda and who was subsequently given a home in the community. The failure of Caedmon's relics to attract pilgrims to Whitby was one of the reasons for the monks' deliberate revival of other cults soon after their return to the abbey

Bergu *(d after 680)*: A nun of Hackness 'who for thirty or more years had been dedicated to the Lord in virginity and had served Him in monastic life' and who, according to Bede, had a vision of Abbess Hilda's soul, on the day of the saint's death, borne to Heaven 'attended and guided by angels'. Bergu's bones, found and identified at Hackness by the monks of Whitby early in the twelfth century, were brought to the abbey to join other relics similarly 'rediscovered' at that time and to bring prosperity, in pilgrims' donations, to the monks.

Trumwin *(d about 700)*: Formerly bishop of Abercorn, on the Firth of Forth, but forced to flee from there in 685 after the death in battle of his patron, King Egfrith. Following this, Bede tells us, Bishop Trumwin 'commended his own people to his friends in such monasteries as he could find and chose his own place of retirement in the monastery, so often mentioned, of the servants and handmaidens of God which is called Whitby. There, with a few of his own people, he lived for many years a life of austerity in the monastery to the benefit of many others'.

Enfleda *(d 704)*: Daughter of Edwin (above) and wife of King Oswy *(d 670)*. After Oswy's death, Enfleda retired to Whitby as a nun, becoming abbess in succession to St Hilda. Oswy himself was buried at Whitby, and it was during Enfleda's abbacy that King Edwin's relics were translated there, to be rated among the community's chief treasures.

A page from an eleventh-century illuminated manuscript of Caedmon's poems, showing Adam and Eve in the Garden of Eden

Bosa *(d 705)*: A former monk of Whitby and 'man of great holiness and humility', who became bishop of York in the intervals of Wilfrid's exiles (678-86 and 691-705).

Wilfrid *(d 709)*: Bishop of York and leading figure in the Christian settlement of the North. Wilfrid was present, as a comparatively young man, at the Synod of Whitby (664) where it was his eloquence that won the day for the Roman party. In a stormy career which was nevertheless highly productive in conversions, Wilfrid quarrelled with almost every other prominent churchman of his time, resulting in lengthy periods of exile.

Elfleda *(d 714)*: Daughter of King Oswy and dedicated to religion by her father following his defeat in battle of the heathen Penda of Mercia. Elfleda was brought up by Abbess Hilda, first at Hartlepool and then at Whitby of which she remained a nun, becoming abbess there in succession to her mother, Enfleda (above). It was Elfleda, 'comforter and best counsellor of the whole province', who achieved the final reconciliation (705) of St Wilfrid with the English Church, and who was also a close friend of St Cuthbert.

Thirteenth-century seal of Hartlepool Abbey showing St Hilda

Mission to the North

Whitby's desolation, two centuries later, was to be the inspiration for its rebirth. Throughout the intervening years, the record of Northumbrian monasticism's greatest period had been kept alive in the writings of its historian, Bede. There were few literate men in Anglo-Saxon England who did not feel the loss as a reproach.

Stephen (d 1112), first abbot of St Mary's, York, an early offshoot of the community at Whitby

Silver-bronze cross excavated at Whitby

Norman energy brought about a revival. Reinfrid, one of William of Normandy's own knights, is known to have visited Whitby soon after the Conquest. It was the sad spectacle of Whitby's ruins that converted Reinfrid to a life of religion, and which led, within a very few years, to a new wave of monastic colonisations in the North.

It was from Evesham (Worcestershire), a rich Anglo-Saxon house still, at that time, under the direction of an Englishman, Abbot Ethelwig, that Reinfrid set out in 1073-74 with two companions, Aldwin and Elfwig, to visit the northern shrines they had each rediscovered in Bede's *Ecclesiastical History of the English People*, and to settle there in solitude and holy peace. The example of these monks was compelling, and they were not left for long by themselves. Never at a loss for recruits, they settled first at Jarrow, Bede's former abode, later taking in Jarrow's sister-house at Wearmouth. By the late 1070s, Reinfrid was back at Whitby, and the work of restoration had begun.

Although many of their adherents were monks from the South, Reinfrid and his companions enjoyed great success in the North. Part of this they owed to a continuing sense of Northumbrian regional identity and traditions, which focused on the cult of St Cuthbert. Celebrated by Bede, Cuthbert of Lindisfarne (634-87) both was and remained the North's most popular saint, his incorruptible body preserved at Durham as a relic of enormous significance. Yet the post-Conquest missionaries brought contributions of their own. Aldwin, especially, was a remarkable teacher, described by a contemporary, Symeon of Durham, as 'patient in adversity, modest in prosperity, acute and provident, weighty in word and deed, always yearning towards heavenly things, and taking thither such as would follow him'. Many indeed, did follow him towards these goals. Moreover, they built with great industry in the effort to secure them, not just at the great cathedral at Durham, that mighty monument to the irreversible drive of the Anglo-Norman settlement, but more modestly at Whitby as well.

The Daily Round - the Horarium

The life of the Benedictine monk was regulated by the *Rule of St Benedict*, dating to the early sixth century. The rule established the pattern of daily life within an Italian monastery, ordering the hours to be used for prayer, spiritual reading and manual work, and setting a timetable for each activity.

The exact hours St Benedict intended for his routine are difficult to establish. They were, in any event, more suitable for a Mediterranean than a northern climate, and were frequently modified in the North. Broadly, northern monks rose for **Matins** shortly after two in the morning. Returning to their beds for a brief rest, they would be woken again for **Lauds** at about five. 'When they rise for the work of God', St Benedict wrote, 'let them gently encourage one another, on account of the excuses to which the sleepy are addicted.' **Prime** coincided with dawn, and might have to be awaited in the choir. It was followed by **Terce** at about eight, by **Sext** at noon, by **None** before two, by **Vespers** in the late afternoon or early evening (say half-past four), and by **Compline** at six (or sunset) before retiring to the dormitory and bed.

In the intervals, Benedictine monks usually read privately in the cloister from Prime until Terce. They met in the chapter house for business and spiritual correction after Terce, and would follow that with a period of work in the library or garden before assembling in the choir again for Sext. The main meal of the day was usually taken after None, at about two. It was followed by a second stretch of private reading until Vespers, by (in the summer) another meal at five, and by the short final service at Compline.

More pauses for refreshment, with a richer and more varied diet, were commonly introduced in later years. Indeed, in the last centuries of English monasticism, social drinking after Compline especially, although in direct contravention of St Benedict's instructions, was so usual as to be ranked among the lesser misdemeanours. In addition, a fair proportion of the monks in a well-off community like Whitby would have had other duties - on the estates, in the library, in the abbey's workshops and its stores - which relieved them from the full round of choir attendance.

Without this, the routine (especially for those with no vocation) could undoubtedly have been crushing to the spirit. Among diseases judged peculiar to the cloister was the deadly lethargy known as 'accidie', part ennui and part melancholia, definable more simply as sloth. Benedict himself had recognised the danger - 'Idleness is the enemy of the soul,' he had pronounced, 'the brethren, therefore, must be occupied at stated hours in manual labour, and again at other hours in sacred reading.'

But Benedict had written for an early elite which, at the frontiers of monasticism, would have assessed his Rule as the moderate programme that the saint indeed intended for his time. Later monks, as the English abbots would one day confess, could not measure up to such demands.

A page from the earliest manuscript of the Rule of St Benedict, c 700

The Wheel of the Religious Life: a virtuous monk ascends to the right of the abbot (top), while a transgressor is cast down to the abbot's left

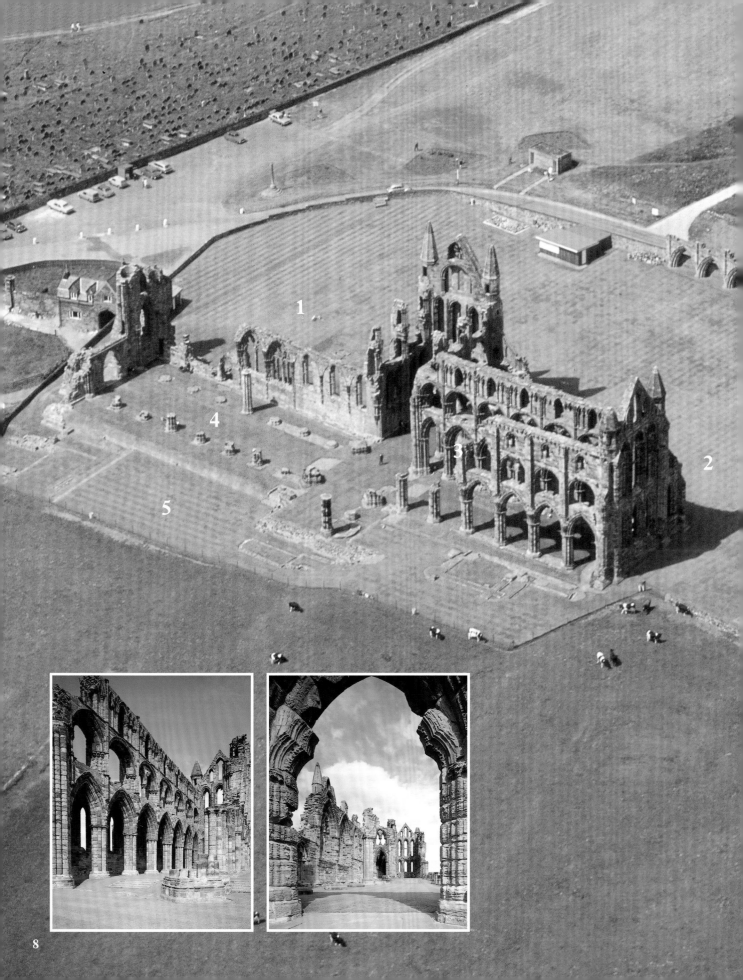

Tour of Whitby Abbey

1 Whitby's story begins here. Under the grass, as revealed by excavation in the 1920s, are the former quarters of the ninth-century Anglo-Saxon nuns. They included several small cell-like buildings, with one larger hall or dormitory to the north. Many objects of interest were recovered from this area, including pins, buckles, tweezers and combs, some of which are illustrated in this guide. The three arches in the precinct wall to the north belong properly to the abbey church, being reconstructions of collapsed arches from the nave (see the Glossary).

2 Look back on the abbey from this point. The fine east front is Whitby's most photographed aspect. It dates to a rebuilding of the 1220s probably associated with the developing cult of Whitby's saints. The three tiers of narrow, pointed (lancet) windows are typical of early Gothic work - a pattern repeated in many buildings of similar scale and date, and in the best contemporary taste.

3 To appreciate the scale of the thirteenth-century rebuilding, stand just about where the monks had their choir stalls. Under your feet are the foundations (see the plan on page 11) of the much shorter and narrower presbytery or easternmost part of the church, built by Reinfrid and his successors in the late eleventh century. It had the characteristic multi-apsed plan of its period, and must have been handsome in its time. Nevertheless, by the early thirteenth century it had come to seem too cramped. It was replaced at great cost by the present aisled presbytery, a building conceived in the grandest of manners. Above the multi-shafted piers is a splendid triforium, and the ornament is carried up further into the blind arcading between the window openings (clerestory) under the roof. This is work of high quality in the best Early English style, typical of the North and paralleled at Rievaulx Abbey in a presbytery enlargement almost exactly contemporary with Whitby's.

4 So expensive was the abbey church's reconstruction that it proceeded only slowly, with many halts for financial recuperation along the way. What you can see of the nave, after its three easternmost bays, is mainly work of the early fourteenth century. Most of this part of the abbey church

collapsed in 1762. What survives of the north wall includes a door and two windows in ornate fourteenth-century decorated style.

Another contemporary door, in the west front, was formerly surmounted by a big Perpendicular window - a typical insertion of the fifteenth century, when modifications to the church still continued. The south wall, adjoining the former cloister, has gone completely, though the pier-bases of the nave arcade are intact.

5 Little survives of the domestic buildings of Whitby Abbey. You are now standing in what was once a cloister, formerly surrounded by ranges of buildings, of which the east held the chapter house (with dormitory over), the south was the refectory or dining hall, and the west contained the kitchen, stores and lodgings. While the church was left intact (though roofless) at the Suppression, probably because of its value as a sea-mark, the remaining abbey buildings immediately lost their purpose, to become a quarry for builders in the locality. Much medieval stonework was re-used in the seventeenth-century Abbey House, an impressive monument just a short distance away to the south west. Abbey House was built by the Cholmley family, who had acquired the monastery precinct in 1540 and who continued to live there for many generations, until their removal to Howsham in the East Riding. Its Banqueting Hall, which is the building you can see across the field, is an addition of the 1670s, strikingly classical in style.

The Abbey Church

Reinfrid did not begin with an empty site. At Whitby, the abbey's chronicler relates, 'there were at that time... as aged countrymen have informed us, *monasteria* or oratories to nearly the number of forty, whereof the walls and altars, empty and roofless, had survived the destruction of the pirate host.' These, indeed, were the ruins that had once affected Reinfrid so deeply. But whereas an Anglo-Saxon, mindful of their associations, might have been tempted to preserve such holy relics, the Norman Reinfrid swept them away.

Everywhere, his own countrymen's reaction was the same. Normandy itself had only recently experienced a monastic reform which had brought it into the van of western monasticism. Accompanying this reform, a new standardised church architecture had developed, influenced by such great continuing projects as the abbey church at Cluny (Burgundy), and commonly characterised by semicircular eastern terminations of the chancel and its chapels now known in the literature as apses. Under the turf of Whitby's thirteenth-century choir and presbytery, the foundations of a first post-Conquest abbey church of exactly this plan have been preserved. By the early twelfth century, if not there before, a standard Benedictine church, with uniform cloister to the south, had replaced the clustered cells and chapels of the saints.

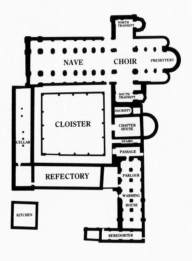

This simplified plan of Thetford Priory, Norfolk, shows the typical layout of a twelfth-century monastery. The original post-Conquest church and cloister at Whitby would have been laid out on similar lines

Whitby's wealth

Although itself smaller than the building that succeeded it, Reinfrid's church would certainly have been grander than the churches or chapels of Abbess Hilda. In an Anglo-Saxon monastic precinct, churches had usually been plentiful - three or more to each community, but they had been small whereas the Norman instinct was to build large.

Whitby was lucky, furthermore, in its early patrons. After Reinfrid, Whitby's next prior was to be Serlo de Percy, brother of William de Percy, the great landowner who had conferred the site and its supporting estate on the new community. Abbot William, Serlo's successor, was himself the founder's nephew. This strong family connection, as had happened before in Elfleda's abbacy, guaranteed the monks' early prosperity. To William de Percy's original donation in the immediate vicinity of their house, Whitby's Benedictines quickly added major estates to the south, towards Scarborough, and to the north, round the nucleus of a dependent priory at Middlesbrough. Rents were rising in the twelfth and thirteenth centuries, wages were low, harvests were good, and the price of agricultural products held firm. Among landowners, a mood of optimism existed.

Whitby had another important financial resource in the flourishing cult of its many saints. There was never a time in the pre-Reformation North when St Hilda, in particular,

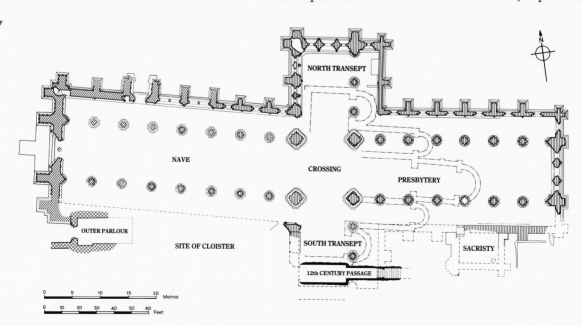

Plan of the existing remains at Whitby, showing the underlying twelfth-century apsed east end

View from the west showing the nave, reconstructed in the fourteenth century, and the east end

was without her devotees. Their loyalty gave the abbots courage to embark on a rebuilding which was one of the most ambitious in the region. In the 1220s Abbot Roger laid out the great choir and presbytery we still see today, setting a new scale for the entire building. The east end at Whitby, a glorious composition in the purest Early English style, was to be a fitting home for the celebration of the saints and for that round of devotions, as regular and predictable as the progress of the sun, which was the major justification of the community.

The abbey in debt

At the end of the thirteenth century, the reputation of Whitby still stood high. It was a house where the Rule of St Benedict was held to be observed '*salubriter et stricte*', and to which others might be sent for correction. Yet the abbey had troubles of its own. Abbot Roger had set an impossible task for his successors. In the late 1250s, the completion of Whitby's crossing and transepts, west of the new presbytery, drove the abbey deep into debt. It was in debt again in the 1320s, at least partly as a result of the beginning then made on a total reconstruction of the nave. The final touches on the church, including the insertion of a great west window in the Perpendicular style, are datable no earlier than the fifteenth century.

Suppression

In the meantime, other matters had gone seriously awry. The Black Death, coming to Whitby in 1349, had taken its toll of the community. Over the country as a whole, a shortage of labour, persisting from that time, inspired a mood of faction and dissent among the tenantry. Wages rose and rents collapsed. Even the weather took a turn for the worse. At Whitby the community soon showed the strain. In a celebrated impasse of the mid 1360s, thought by many to be beyond resolution, some took the side of an extravagant and dictatorial abbot, others of a corrupt and indulgent prior. There were allegations of incontinence and private property at the abbey. The king himself had to be called in to give judgement.

Watercolour of the ruins of Whitby Abbey by J C Buckler (d 1894)

Deliberately, in their later years, the abbots of Whitby maintained a reduced establishment. After the Black Death, recruitment at the community never rose again to the forty or so monks of its twelfth-century maximum, usually standing at barely half that figure, with about the same number of in-house servants. Of course, a good deal of the purpose of retrenchment of this kind was to ensure that the survivors should live well. When, in 1521-22, the call came for a thorough going spring-clean of the 'black monk' houses, the Benedictine abbots' response to Cardinal Wolsey's criticisms was that few, in their time, had a taste for austerity and that recruitment, already slack, might reasonably be expected to fall off altogether if the strict letter of the Rule were enforced.

The attack on the monasteries

Henry VIII's break with Rome, following the Pope's refusal to support his divorce from Catherine of Aragon, left the English monasteries vulnerable to attack. Low in esteem, but still in many cases comfortably off, the religious houses - Whitby among them - promised rich pickings to the king and to his predatory local gentry, already much involved in their affairs. The first assault, in 1536, involved the suppression or closure of the smaller houses, defined as those with an income of £200 or less. Whitby, with a yield of £437 on its estates, comfortably exceeded the stated minimum.

Henry's foreign wars were proving increasingly expensive, and the remaining 'greater' monasteries were steadily steered into 'voluntary surrenders'. At Whitby, the vultures quickly gathered. Certainly the worst of these was the 'insatiable' Gregory Conyers, who 'hath the most living of our house of any man' and whose conduct contributed to the voluntary resignation, in his old age and feebleness, of Whitby's penultimate abbot. However, it was not to Conyers that the abbey's site descended after the community's formal surrender to the king's commissioners - almost the last among the great houses - in mid-December 1539. Leased on 2 March 1540 to

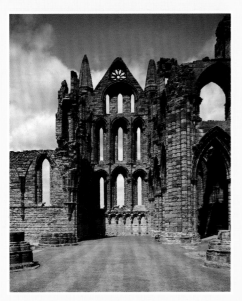

The north transept

The Act of 1536.....

The following extracts from the Act of 1536, dissolving the lesser houses and pensioning off their inmates, usefully convey the Government's first intentions which did not, at that time, extend to the outright suppression (later achieved by the 'voluntary surrenders' of 1538-40) of every monastic community in the kingdom.

Richard Cholmley, another local man, the entire precinct was purchased by him some fifteen years later and long remained in the hands of his kin.

The Cholmley mansion, several times rebuilt out of materials largely plundered from the dissolved monastery, survives as a roofless shell to the south west. It is an interesting building in its own right, especially for the former banqueting hall (clearly visible from the abbey ruins) which retains an impressive classical façade of the 1670s. Its construction had been achieved at great cost. At Whitby now, scarcely anything remains of the three ranges of the cloister - chapter house and dormitory to the east, refectory to the south, abbot's lodgings and guesthouse to the west - which once sheltered against the south façade of the great church. There in the cloister, protected from the chill sea breeze, Whitby's monks perused devotional works - perhaps a life of St Hilda or the *Ecclesiastical History* of Bede - in little studies (carrels) of their own. They assembled at the appointed hours for worship in the choir. Released from their duties, they gathered regularly for conversation or refreshment in warming house or refectory, before retiring to the dormitory until Matins. While other men made war and still more tilled the land, the monks kept their eyes on salvation. It was a role gladly accepted by those for whom they prayed, to come in question only when abused.

The ruins of the abbey in 1789, before the collapse of the central tower and west front

FORASMUCH as manifest sin, vicious, carnal, and abominable living is daily used and committed among the little and small abbeys, priories, and other religious houses of monks, canons, and nuns, where the congregation of such religious persons is under the number of twelve persons...and albeit that many continual visitations hath been heretofore had, by the space of two hundred years and more, for an honest and charitable reformation of such unthrifty, carnal, and abominable living, yet nevertheless little or none amendment is hitherto had, but their vicious living shamelessly increases and augment....

IN consideration whereof the king's most royal majesty, being supreme head on earth under God of the Church of England, daily finding and devising the increase, advancement, and exaltation of true doctrine and virtue in the said Church, to the only glory and honour of God and the total extirping and destruction of vice and sin, having knowledge that the premises be true, as well by the accounts of his late visitations as by sundry credible information, considering also that divers and great solemn monasteries of this realm wherein (thanks be to God) religion is right well kept and observed, be destitute of such full numbers of religious persons as they ought and may keep, has thought that a plain declaration should be made of the premises, as well as to the Lords spiritual and temporal as to other his loving subjects the Commons in this present Parliament assembled.

WHEREUPON the said Lords and commons, by a great deliberation, finally be resolved that it is and shall be much more to the pleasure of Almighty God and for the honour of this his realm that the possessions of such small religious houses, now being spent, spoiled, and wasted for increase and maintenance of sin, should be used and converted to better uses and the unthrifty religious persons so spending the same to be compelled to reform their lives: and thereupon most humbly desire the king's highness that it may enacted by authority of this present Parliament that his majesty shall have and enjoy to him and his heirs forever all and singular such monasteries...which have not in lands, tenements, rents, tithes, portions, and other hereditaments, above the clear yearly value of two hundred pounds. And in like manner shall have and enjoy all the sites and circuits of every such religious house and all and singular the manors, granges, meases, lands, tenements, rents, reversions, services, tithes, pensions, portions, churches, chapels, advowsons, patronages, annuities, rights, entries, conditions, and other hereditaments appertaining or belonging to every such monastery, priory, or other religious houses in as large and ample manner as the abbots now have, or ought to, have the same in the right of their houses....

IN consideration of which premises to be had to his highness and to his heirs as is aforesaid, his majesty is pleased and contented, of his most excellent charity, to provide to every chief head and governor of every such religious house, during their lives, such yearly pensions and benefices as for their degrees and qualities shall be reasonable and convenient...and also his majesty will ordain and provide that the convents of every such religious house shall have their capacities, if they will, to live honestly and virtuously abroad, and some convenient charity disposed to them towards their living, or else shall be committed to such honourable great monasteries of this realm wherein good religion is observed, as shall be limited by his highness, there to live religiously during their lives.

Glossary

Apse - the semicircular termination of a chancel or chapel at its eastern end, usually holding the altar

Arcade - a series of columns (piers) supporting arches

Bay - the division of a building, as marked by a unit of vaulting etc

Benedictine - monks who, observing the Rule of St Benedict of Monte Cassino (*d* 550), were first brought together under a collective discipline by St Benedict of Aniane in 817

Blind Arcade - blank arches carried on columns and set against the wall as a decorative device, as at clerestory level at Whitby

Chancel - the eastern arm of a church, usually reserved to the clergy

Chapter house - the chamber, usually sited centrally in the east claustral range, where the monks met daily for business and instruction, including the reading of a chapter of the Rule

Choir - the part of the church, from the crossing into the presbytery, where the choir stalls of the monks were placed

Clerestory - the top line of windows, under the roof (at Whitby, on the third tier), helping to light the body of a church

Cloister - an open space adjoining the church, square in plan and surrounded by a galleried passage, used by the monks for exercise and study

Crossing - the intersection of nave, transepts, and chancel

Decorated - the term usually given in England to the second phase of Gothic (1275-1350), characterised by ambitious and inventive window tracery and by much use of surface decoration on architectural elements of all kind

Dormitory - the common sleeping chamber of the monks, usually on the first floor of the east range of the cloister where it could be directly accessible (by night stair) from the church

Early English - the first phase of unadulterated Gothic in England, familiar from about 1200, characterised by pointed lancet windows

Nave - the western arm of a church, usually its main body, intended to give space for a congregation

Perpendicular - the last and most English of the Gothic styles, first introduced in the mid fourteenth century and characterised by straight tracery and large windows

Pier - a column supporting the arches of an arcade

Precinct - the enclosure, usually walled, surrounding and including a monastic or other large church

Presbytery - the part of the church, beyond the choir and to the east, containing the high altar and major shrines

Refectory - the common eating chamber (dining hall) of the monks

Transept - the transverse arm, north or south, of a cruciform church

Triforium - the arcade, usually purely decorative, above the nave arcade and below the clerestory

Warming house - the common chamber where the monks could warm themselves by the fire

Key Dates

597	Augustine, sent by Pope Gregory, reaches England; he is made bishop of Canterbury
612-33	Edwin, King of Northumbria (later St Edwin)
654-70	Oswy, King of Northumbria
655	Oswy defeats and kills Penda of Mercia at Winwaed; he has vowed to found twelve monasteries and to dedicate his daughter , Elfleda, to religion
657	Hilda comes to Whitby and establishes a double monastery there
664	Synod of Whitby: Oswy decides in favour of the Roman (against the Celtic) rite
680	Death of St Hilda; succeeded by Enfleda (*d 704*), Oswy's queen, and Elfleda (*d 714*), his daughter; important relics are brought to Whitby
731	Bede finishes his *Ecclesiastical History of the English People*
867	The Danes sack Whitby; monastic life ceases there for two centuries
1066-87	William the Conqueror, King of England and Duke of Normandy
1073-74	The Mission to the North: Reinfrid, Aldwin and Elfwig set out from Evesham Abbey to visit and restore the northern shrines
1078	Reinfrid re-establishes monastic life at Whitby; work on the first post-Conquest church begins
c 1125	The monks of Whitby 'discover' and rehouse their saints
c 1220	Work starts on the new presbytery at Whitby
1250-60	Completion of the crossing and transepts
c 1320	Reconstruction of the main body of the nave begins
1349	The Black Death comes to Whitby
1365-66	Dispute at Whitby; the majority sides with the prior against the abbot
1521-22	Cardinal Wolsey seeks to reform the Benedictine ('black monk') houses, but is told by their abbots that it is too late to return to the letter of the Rule
1536	Suppression of the lesser houses (those with income below £200)
1538-40	Suppression of the greater houses, including Whitby (14 December 1539)
1540	The abbey site and precinct are leased (2 March) to Richard Cholmley, who purchases the freehold on 2 July 1555